AI
Artificial
Intelligence

In
EDUCATION

"The Impact of Artificial Intelligence on Education"

Book By: B. WATKINS

Introduction:

Artificial intelligence (AI) is revolutionizing various industries and transforming the way we live and work. In recent years, AI has also made its way into education, offering the potential to transform the way students learn and teachers teach. AI in education refers to the use of AI technologies, such as machine learning, natural language processing, and computer vision, to enhance and personalize the learning experience. The use of AI in education can enable personalized learning, real-time feedback, adaptive teaching, and automation of administrative tasks. AI-powered education technologies can also help educators identify students' learning gaps and provide them with targeted interventions to address these gaps. Despite the potential benefits, there are also concerns about the ethical implications and limitations of using AI in education. As such, it is crucial to carefully consider the role of AI in education and how it can be used to benefit students and teachers alike.

Summary:

AI in education refers to the use of artificial intelligence technology to enhance teaching and learning. AI-powered education technologies can provide personalized learning experiences for each student, adapt to their individual learning styles, and provide real-time feedback. The use of AI in education can improve learning outcomes, enhance teacher effectiveness, and increase student engagement. However, educators play a critical role in designing and implementing AI-powered education technologies, interpreting and analyzing learning data, and providing social and emotional support to students. The use of AI in education must be done in a way that enhances, not replaces, human interaction. Successful applications of AI in education include Duolingo, Carnegie Learning, Coursera, and Dreambox.

Table of Contents

History of AI in Education: From Early Attempts to Current State

Artificial Intelligence (AI) is changing the world in profound ways, and education is no exception. AI has the potential to revolutionize the way we teach and learn, making education more accessible, personalized, and effective. However, the history of AI in education is not without its challenges and limitations. In this article, we will explore the history of AI in education, from early attempts to the current state of the field.

Early Attempts at AI in Education

The idea of using computers to enhance learning can be traced back to the 1960s when the first computer-based educational systems were developed. These early systems were simple and primarily focused on drill and practice exercises. They were not intelligent in the sense that we understand AI today, but they paved the way for more sophisticated systems.

In the 1970s and 1980s, the field of AI began to develop rapidly, and researchers began exploring the potential of AI in education. One of the earliest attempts at AI in education was the Intelligent Tutoring System (ITS), developed at Carnegie Mellon University. The ITS was designed to provide students with personalized feedback and guidance, much like a human tutor.

Another significant development in the field of AI in education during this period was the creation of expert systems. These systems were designed to replicate the decision-making processes of human experts in a particular domain. For example, an expert system might be created to help students learn how to diagnose medical conditions.

Despite these early attempts, AI in education remained a niche area of research until the early 2000s when advances in technology and machine learning algorithms made it more feasible.

Current State of AI in Education

Today, AI is being used in a variety of ways to enhance teaching and learning. Some of the most promising applications of AI in education include adaptive learning systems, intelligent tutoring systems, automated essay grading, and personalized learning environments.

Adaptive Learning Systems

Adaptive learning systems use machine learning algorithms to analyze student data and provide personalized learning experiences. These systems can adapt to a student's individual learning style, pace, and knowledge level, providing them with the right content and activities to help them learn.

Intelligent Tutoring Systems

Intelligent tutoring systems are designed to provide students with personalized feedback and guidance, much like a human tutor. These systems use machine learning algorithms to analyze student data and provide tailored instruction and support.

Automated Essay Grading

Automated essay grading uses machine learning algorithms to grade student essays. This technology can provide immediate feedback to students, helping them improve their writing skills.

Personalized Learning Environments

Personalized learning environments use AI to create customized learning experiences for students. These environments can adapt to a student's individual learning style, preferences, and pace, providing them with the right content and activities to help them learn.

Challenges and Limitations of AI in Education

Despite AI's promise in education, there are several obstacles and constraints to consider. One of the most difficult difficulties is the requirement for massive volumes of data. Because AI algorithms rely on data to learn, they may be unable to deliver correct insights or suggestions if there is insufficient data.

Another issue is the requirement for human supervision. While artificial intelligence can give useful insights and recommendations, it cannot replace the human touch. Teachers and educators are still necessary for offering direction, support, and mentorship to pupils.

Additionally, there are concerns about the potential for bias and discrimination in AI. Machine learning algorithms can replicate and amplify existing biases, perpetuating inequalities in education.

Ethics and Privacy Concerns in AI Education

Another area of concern is ethics and privacy. AI algorithms can collect large amounts of data about students, including their learning preferences, behaviors, and academic performance. This data can be used to create personalized learning experiences, but it can also be misused or mishandled, raising concerns about privacy and security.

There are also ethical considerations when it comes to using AI in education. For example, there are questions about the use of AI in grading and assessment. Some argue that AI cannot replicate the complex, nuanced decision-making processes of human graders, and that relying on AI could be unfair or inaccurate.

Future of AI in Education

Despite these challenges and limitations, the future of AI in education looks bright. As technology continues to advance, AI will become more powerful and more widely used in education. Some experts predict that AI could completely transform education, making it more accessible, personalized, and effective than ever before.

One potential area of growth for AI in education is STEM education. AI can help students learn complex concepts and skills in areas like math, science, and engineering. For example, AI-powered simulations and games could help students learn physics or chemistry in a more engaging and interactive way.

Another area of growth is language learning. AI-powered language learning tools could help students learn new languages faster and more effectively, providing them with personalized feedback and support.

Implementing AI in Education: Best Practices and Strategies

To effectively implement AI in education, it is important to follow best practices and strategies. These include:

1. Starting small: Begin by piloting AI in a single classroom or subject area before scaling up.
2. Ensuring data privacy and security: Develop clear policies and procedures for collecting, storing, and using student data.
3. Providing teacher training: Teachers need to be trained on how to use AI effectively

and how to integrate it into their teaching practice.
4. Encouraging collaboration: AI should be used as a tool to enhance collaboration between teachers, students, and parents.
5. Continuously evaluating and iterating: Regularly evaluate the effectiveness of AI in education and make adjustments as needed.

Successful Applications of AI in Education

There are many successful applications of AI in education. One example is Carnegie Learning, a company that provides AI-powered adaptive learning systems for math education. The company's systems use machine learning algorithms to analyze student data and provide personalized learning experiences.

Another successful application is Gradescope, an AI-powered grading tool that provides instant feedback on student work. The tool uses machine learning algorithms to analyze student work and provide instant feedback, helping students improve their writing skills.

Theoretical Frameworks for AI in Education

As AI continues to gain prominence in the field of education, researchers and educators alike have been exploring theoretical frameworks for understanding and leveraging AI in the classroom. In this article, we will explore several key theoretical frameworks for AI in education, including cognitive load theory, constructivism, and the zone of proximal development.

Cognitive Load Theory

Cognitive load theory is a framework that helps us understand how the brain processes and learns new information. According to this theory, the brain has a limited capacity for processing information, and learning is most effective when cognitive load is managed in a way that optimizes working memory.

In the context of AI in education, cognitive load theory has important implications for how we design educational materials and interactions. AI can be used to reduce cognitive load by providing personalized learning experiences that are tailored to the individual needs and abilities of each student. For example, an AI-powered tutoring system can adapt to a student's level of knowledge and provide targeted feedback and support to help them manage their cognitive load more effectively.

Constructivism

Constructivism is a learning theory that emphasizes the importance of active, experiential learning in which learners construct their own understanding of the world through their experiences and interactions with the environment. In this framework, learning is seen as a process of constructing meaning, rather than passively receiving information.

In the context of AI in education, constructivism has important implications for how we design learning experiences that engage learners in active, experiential learning. AI can be used to create interactive learning experiences that allow students to explore and experiment with new concepts and ideas, rather than simply receiving information in a passive way. For example, an AI-powered virtual lab can allow students to simulate real-world experiments and explore scientific concepts in a hands-on way.

The zone of proximal development is a framework developed by psychologist Lev Vygotsky to describe the difference between what a learner can do on their own and what they can do with the help of a more knowledgeable other. According to this framework, learning is most effective when it occurs in the zone of proximal development, where learners are challenged to stretch beyond their current level of knowledge and skill, but not so far beyond that they become frustrated or overwhelmed.

In the context of AI in education, the zone of proximal development has important implications for how we design educational interactions that challenge learners to grow and develop their skills. AI can be used to provide targeted support and feedback to help learners operate within their zone of proximal development, and to scaffold their learning in a way that helps them gradually build toward mastery of a given skill or concept.

In addition to the three frameworks discussed above, there are several other theoretical frameworks that are relevant to AI in education.

Let's explore a few of these frameworks in more detail:

Social Learning Theory

Social learning theory, developed by psychologist Albert Bandura, emphasizes the importance of social interactions and modeling in the learning process. According to this theory, people learn by observing the behavior of others and the consequences of those behaviors. This can be particularly relevant in the context of AI in education, as AI-powered virtual assistants or chatbots can be designed to model positive behaviors and provide examples for students to follow.

Self-Determination Theory

Self-determination theory, developed by psychologists Edward Deci and Richard Ryan, is a framework that emphasizes the importance of autonomy, competence, and relatedness in motivation and learning. According to this theory, learners are most motivated and engaged when they feel that they have control over their learning environment, are capable of achieving their goals, and are connected to others who share their interests and values. In the context of AI in education, this theory suggests that AI can be used to personalize learning experiences and give students more control over their own learning, helping to increase their motivation and engagement.

Connectivism

Connectivism is a learning theory that emphasizes the importance of networks and connections in the learning process. According to this theory, learning is a process of connecting nodes of information and ideas, rather than simply acquiring knowledge or skills. In the context of AI in education, this theory suggests that AI can be used to facilitate connections between learners, teachers, and resources, creating a networked learning environment that supports collaborative learning and knowledge creation.

Ecological Systems Theory

Ecological systems theory, developed by psychologist Urie Bronfenbrenner, is a framework that emphasizes the importance of the social and environmental contexts in which learning takes place. According to this theory, learners are influenced by multiple levels of context, from the individual level to the societal level. In the context of AI in education, this theory suggests that AI can be used to create personalized learning experiences that take into account the unique social and environmental contexts of each learner, helping to create a more supportive and inclusive learning environment.

Overall, these theoretical frameworks provide valuable insights into how we can design AI-powered educational interactions that are effective, engaging, and supportive of student learning and development. By leveraging these frameworks, educators can help their students take full advantage of the potential of AI to enhance their learning and help them achieve their full potential.

Benefits of AI in Education: Improving Learning Outcomes

Artificial intelligence (AI) is rapidly transforming the landscape of education, offering new possibilities for personalized, adaptive, and data-driven learning. From intelligent tutoring systems to chatbots and grading automation, AI-powered tools are helping to improve learning outcomes in a variety of ways. In this article, we'll explore some of the key benefits of AI in education and how they can contribute to better learning outcomes for students.

Personalized Learning

One of the most significant benefits of AI in education is its ability to personalize learning experiences for individual students. By analyzing data on student performance, engagement, and preferences, AI-powered systems can adapt content, pace, and feedback to meet the needs of each learner. This can help students to stay motivated, engaged, and challenged, while also supporting their strengths and addressing their weaknesses. Research has shown that personalized learning can lead to higher academic achievement, better retention of information, and increased student engagement and satisfaction.

Adaptive Learning

Adaptive learning is another important benefit of AI in education. By using machine learning algorithms to analyze data on student performance and progress, adaptive learning systems can adjust the difficulty, sequence, and content of learning activities to match each student's level of knowledge and skill. This can help to prevent boredom and frustration, while also providing students with a more challenging and engaging learning experience. Research has shown that adaptive learning can lead to significant improvements in student achievement, particularly in subjects such as math and science.

Instant Feedback

AI-powered tools can also provide instant feedback to students, allowing them to assess their understanding and identify areas for improvement in real time. For example, chatbots and virtual tutors can engage students in conversations and ask them questions to help them clarify their understanding of concepts.

Automated grading systems can provide immediate feedback on written assignments, allowing students to learn from their mistakes and improve their writing skills. Instant feedback can help students to stay on track and make continuous progress, without the need to wait for a teacher's feedback.

Data-Driven Decision Making

Another benefit of AI in education is its ability to collect and analyze data on student learning and performance. By tracking student progress and identifying patterns in their behavior, AI-powered tools can help educators to make data-driven decisions about instructional strategies, curriculum design, and student support. For example, an intelligent tutoring system can track student progress and generate reports for teachers, highlighting areas where students are struggling and suggesting targeted interventions to address these issues. Data-driven decision making can help educators to optimize learning outcomes and ensure that each student receives the support they need to succeed.

Time Savings

AI-powered tools can also save educators time and reduce administrative burden, allowing them to focus on teaching and supporting their students. Automated grading systems, for example, can significantly reduce the time required to grade assignments, freeing up teachers to provide more targeted feedback and support. Chatbots and virtual tutors can also answer common student questions, reducing the need for teachers to respond to these queries individually. By automating routine tasks and providing support for teachers, AI can help to optimize the use of resources and improve the quality of education.

Accessibility

AI-powered tools can also help to make education more accessible and inclusive for students with disabilities or other learning challenges. For example, speech recognition software can help students with speech impairments to communicate more effectively, while text-to-speech software can help students with visual impairments to access written content. Intelligent tutoring systems can also be customized to meet the unique needs of each student, providing additional support and scaffolding as needed. By providing customized support and accommodations, AI can help to ensure that all students have access to high-quality education.

Overall, the benefits of AI in education are many and varied, offering new possibilities for personalized, adaptive, and data-driven learning. By leveraging AI-powered tools, educators can help their students to achieve better learning outcomes, improve their academic achievement, and develop the skills and knowledge they need to succeed in the 21st century. However, it's important to note that AI is not a magic solution, and it's not a substitute for good teaching or human interaction. Rather, AI should be seen as a tool to support and enhance the work of educators, and to help them to provide the best possible learning experiences for their students.

It's also important to consider the potential limitations and challenges of AI in education, including issues related to data privacy, bias, and ethics. As with any technology, AI must be used responsibly and ethically, and educators and policymakers must be mindful of the potential risks and challenges of its use. Nonetheless, when used effectively and responsibly, AI has the potential to revolutionize education and provide new opportunities for students to learn, grow, and succeed.

Challenges and Limitations of AI in Education

While the potential benefits of AI in education are significant, there are also several challenges and limitations that must be addressed in order to maximize its effectiveness and ensure responsible use. These challenges include technical limitations, ethical concerns, and the need for effective implementation strategies.

One of the main technical challenges of AI in education is the need for high-quality data. AI algorithms rely on large amounts of data to learn and make predictions, and if this data is incomplete, inaccurate, or biased, the algorithm's predictions may be flawed. In education, this can be particularly challenging due to the diversity of learners and the complexity of educational contexts. It can be difficult to gather accurate and representative data on student performance, teacher effectiveness, and other key variables, and even when such data is available, it may be difficult to integrate into AI algorithms.

Another technical challenge is the need for effective algorithms that can adapt to changing circumstances and individual learners. While many AI algorithms are capable of making predictions based on historical data, they may struggle to adapt to new situations or account for individual differences in learning styles, interests, and preferences. This can limit their effectiveness in providing personalized learning experiences and may lead to frustration or disengagement among learners.

Ethical concerns are also a major challenge in the use of AI in education. One concern is the potential for bias in AI algorithms, which may perpetuate existing inequalities or stereotypes. For example, an AI algorithm that uses historical data to predict student performance may inadvertently reflect biases in that data, such as gender or racial biases. This could lead to unfair treatment of certain groups of students and perpetuate existing inequalities in education.

Another ethical concern is the potential for AI to replace human teachers or reduce the amount of human interaction in the classroom. While AI can be an effective tool for providing personalized feedback and support, it cannot replace the social and emotional benefits of human interaction. Additionally, there may be concerns around data privacy and the collection and use of student data by AI algorithms. It's important for educators and policymakers to consider these ethical concerns and develop strategies to address them.

Effective implementation of AI in education is also a challenge. AI is a complex technology that requires significant resources, expertise, and infrastructure to implement effectively. Additionally, it can be difficult to integrate AI into existing educational practices and systems, and to ensure that it aligns with broader educational goals and strategies. There may also be resistance to the use of AI among educators, students, and parents, particularly if they feel that it undermines the role of human teachers or reduces the importance of traditional educational practices.

Despite these challenges, there are several strategies that can be used to address them and maximize the effectiveness of AI in education. One approach is to prioritize the ethical use of AI in education, including the development of algorithms that are transparent, accountable, and bias-free. This can involve engaging diverse stakeholders in the design and implementation of AI systems, including educators, students, parents, and community members.

Another strategy is to focus on the development of personalized learning experiences that are tailored to individual learners. This can involve using AI to analyze student data and provide customized feedback and support, as well as providing learners with a range of learning resources and tools that are adapted to their needs and preferences.

Effective implementation of AI in education also requires a focus on teacher professional development and capacity building. Educators need to be trained in the use of AI and supported in its implementation, in order to ensure that it aligns with broader educational goals and strategies. This can involve providing educators with training and resources, as well as developing collaborative partnerships between educators and AI experts.

AI-Powered Adaptive Learning Systems

AI-powered adaptive learning systems are designed to personalize learning for each student based on their individual needs and learning styles. These systems use artificial intelligence (AI) algorithms to analyze student performance data and adapt the learning experience to better meet the needs of each student. This article will explore the benefits and challenges of adaptive learning systems, as well as the different types of AI-powered adaptive learning systems and their potential impact on education.

Benefits of AI-Powered Adaptive Learning Systems

One of the biggest benefits of AI-powered adaptive learning systems is their ability to personalize the learning experience for each student. By analyzing student performance data, these systems can identify areas where a student is struggling and adjust the content and pace of the learning experience to help them succeed. This can help students who are struggling to keep up with their peers to catch up and improve their academic performance.

Another benefit of AI-powered adaptive learning systems is their ability to provide immediate feedback to students. With traditional classroom learning, students may have to wait for days or even weeks to receive feedback on their work. With adaptive learning systems, students receive feedback in real-time, which can help them identify areas where they need to improve and make adjustments to their learning strategies.

Adaptive learning systems can also help to increase student engagement and motivation. By providing a personalized learning experience that is tailored to each student's individual needs and interests, these systems can help students to stay engaged and motivated throughout the learning process. This can help to reduce dropout rates and increase academic achievement.

Challenges of AI-Powered Adaptive Learning Systems

One of the biggest challenges of AI-powered adaptive learning systems is the potential for bias in the algorithms used to analyze student data. If the algorithms are biased, they may make incorrect assumptions about students' abilities or interests, which can lead to inappropriate content or pacing adjustments. This can have a negative impact on student learning outcomes and can reinforce existing inequalities in education.

Another challenge of adaptive learning systems is the potential for students to become too reliant on technology. If students are always receiving immediate feedback and personalized content, they may become less independent in their learning and less able to cope with the demands of traditional classroom environments.

Types of AI-Powered Adaptive Learning Systems

There are several different types of AI-powered adaptive learning systems, each with its own unique features and benefits.

Content-Driven Adaptive Learning Systems

Content-driven adaptive learning systems use AI algorithms to analyze student performance data and adjust the content of the learning experience to better meet the needs of each student. This can include adjusting the difficulty level of the content, providing additional resources or support materials, or offering alternative learning paths to help students who are struggling in a particular area.

Personalized Learning Environments

Personalized learning environments use AI algorithms to create a tailored learning experience for each student based on their individual needs and interests. This can include personalized lesson plans, recommended readings, and other resources that are designed to help each student succeed.

Intelligent Tutoring Systems

Intelligent tutoring systems use AI algorithms to provide individualized support to students as they work through learning activities. This can include providing feedback on incorrect answers, offering hints or suggestions to help students who are struggling, and providing personalized guidance and support to help students achieve their learning goals.

Chatbots and Conversational Agents

Chatbots and conversational agents use AI algorithms to provide students with personalized support and guidance as they work through learning activities. This can include answering questions, providing feedback on incorrect answers, and offering personalized resources and support materials.

3. Impact of AI-Powered Adaptive Learning Systems on Education

AI-powered adaptive learning systems have the potential to revolutionize the way that education is delivered. By providing a personalized learning experience that is tailored to each student's individual needs and interests, these systems can help to improve student engagement, motivation, and academic achievement.

3.1 Types of AI-Powered Adaptive Learning Systems

There are different types of AI-powered adaptive learning systems that can be used in education. Here are some of the most common ones:

3.1. Knowledge Tracing Systems

Knowledge tracing systems are based on Bayesian models that estimate the probability that a student has mastered a specific concept based on their responses to questions. These systems can be used to predict the likelihood of a student's success in a course, provide personalized feedback, and suggest appropriate learning activities.

3.2. Intelligent Tutoring Systems

Intelligent tutoring systems are designed to provide personalized instruction and feedback to students. These systems use AI algorithms to adapt the pace, content, and difficulty level of the learning materials to the individual needs of each student. They can also provide real-time feedback and support to help students overcome difficulties.

3.3. Personalized Learning Environments

Personalized learning environments are online platforms that provide students with customized learning experiences. These platforms use AI algorithms to analyze data on each student's learning progress, interests, and preferences, and to suggest appropriate learning activities and resources. They can also provide real-time feedback and support to help students overcome difficulties.

3.4. Adaptive Assessment Systems

Adaptive assessment systems are designed to provide personalized assessments that adapt to the individual needs and abilities of each student. These systems use AI algorithms to adjust the difficulty level and type of questions based on the student's responses. They can also provide real-time feedback and support to help students improve their performance.

4. Advantages and Disadvantages of AI-Powered Adaptive Learning Systems

AI-powered adaptive learning systems have several advantages over traditional classroom instruction. These are a few examples of the most common:

4.1. Personalized Learning

One of the most significant advantages of AI-powered adaptive learning systems is that they provide personalized learning experiences that are tailored to the individual needs and abilities of each student. This can help students learn more efficiently and effectively, as they can focus on the topics that are most relevant to them and learn at their own pace.

4.2. Real-Time Feedback and Support

AI-powered adaptive learning systems can provide real-time feedback and support to students, which can help them overcome difficulties and improve their performance. This can help students feel more motivated and engaged in their learning, as they can see their progress and receive immediate feedback on their performance.

4.3. Flexibility

AI-powered adaptive learning systems are flexible and can be accessed from anywhere with an internet connection. This means that students can learn at their own pace and on their own schedule, which can be particularly beneficial for students who have other commitments or who prefer to learn outside of traditional classroom settings.

4.4. Cost-Effective

AI-powered adaptive learning systems can be cost-effective, as they can reduce the need for expensive textbooks, classroom materials, and teacher time. This can make education more accessible and affordable for students who might not otherwise have access to high-quality educational resources.

However, there are also some disadvantages to using AI-powered adaptive learning systems in education. These are a few examples of the most common:

4.5. Limited Interpersonal Interaction

AI-powered adaptive learning systems can provide personalized learning experiences, but they cannot replace the interpersonal interaction and socialization that occurs in traditional classroom settings. This can be particularly challenging for students who need more support or who benefit from interacting with teachers and peers.

4.6. Technical Issues

AI-powered adaptive learning systems can be complex and require technical expertise to implement and maintain. This can be a challenge for schools and educators who do not have the resources or technical expertise to implement and maintain these systems effectively.

4.7. Data Privacy and Security

AI-powered adaptive learning systems require access to sensitive student data, which can raise concerns about data privacy and security. Schools and educators must ensure that these systems

One of the challenges of developing adaptive learning systems is the need to collect and analyze large amounts of data. Machine learning algorithms require access to large quantities of data in order to identify patterns and make accurate predictions. This means that adaptive learning systems must be able to collect data on student performance in a variety of contexts, including assessments, homework assignments, and classroom activities.

In addition, adaptive learning systems must be designed with the unique needs of each learner in mind. This requires a deep understanding of the various factors that can influence learning, such as prior knowledge, learning style, and motivation. In order to provide truly personalized learning experiences, adaptive learning systems must be able to analyze a wide range of data points in order to identify patterns and make accurate predictions about each learner's needs.

Another challenge of developing adaptive learning systems is the need to ensure that they are both effective and ethical. While adaptive learning systems have the potential to improve learning outcomes and increase engagement, they must also be designed with the well-being of learners in mind. This means that they must be transparent, explainable, and accountable, and must not perpetuate bias or discrimination.

Despite these challenges, there are a number of successful examples of adaptive learning systems that are already being used in classrooms around the world. For example, Knewton is an adaptive learning platform that uses machine learning algorithms to analyze data on student performance and provide personalized recommendations for learning activities. Another example is Carnegie Learning, which offers an adaptive math curriculum that uses data analytics and machine learning to personalize learning experiences for each student.

AI-Enabled Personalized Learning Environments

Personalized learning has become a buzzword in the education sector, and technology has played a critical role in enabling this concept. Artificial intelligence (AI) is a key component of personalized learning, as it allows for the creation of personalized learning environments that can adapt to the unique needs of individual students. AI-enabled personalized learning environments are becoming increasingly popular in classrooms around the world, and for good reason: they offer a range of benefits for students and educators alike.

In this article, we will explore the concept of AI-enabled personalized learning environments, their benefits, and the challenges associated with their implementation.

What are AI-Enabled Personalized Learning Environments?

AI-enabled personalized learning environments are digital learning environments that use artificial intelligence to adapt to the individual learning needs and preferences of each student.

These environments provide a highly individualized and interactive learning experience, which can significantly improve student engagement and learning outcomes.

The key components of an AI-enabled personalized learning environment include:

1. Adaptive Learning Algorithms: These algorithms use data about the student's learning patterns and preferences to create a personalized learning path that adapts to the student's needs in real-time.
2. Personalized Content: The content is tailored to the student's individual learning needs and preferences, such as their preferred learning style, interests, and abilities.
3. Real-Time Feedback: Students receive immediate feedback on their progress, which helps them to identify areas where they need to improve and adjust their learning strategies accordingly.

Benefits of AI-Enabled Personalized Learning Environments:

1. Increased Engagement: One of the primary benefits of AI-enabled personalized

learning environments is increased student engagement. Students are more likely to stay engaged in the learning process when they are presented with content that is tailored to their individual learning needs and preferences.

2. Improved Learning Outcomes: Personalized learning has been shown to significantly improve learning outcomes. According to a study by the RAND Corporation, students in personalized learning environments made significantly greater gains in math and reading than their peers in traditional classroom settings.

3. Flexibility: AI-enabled personalized learning environments offer a high degree of flexibility, as students can learn at their own pace and on their own schedule. This can be especially beneficial for students who may need extra time or support to master a particular concept.

4. Data-Driven Insights: AI-enabled personalized learning environments generate a wealth of data about student learning patterns and preferences. This data can be used to identify areas where students are struggling, adjust teaching

strategies, and provide targeted interventions.

1. Implementation Costs: Implementing AI-enabled personalized learning environments can be expensive, as it requires significant investments in technology, infrastructure, and personnel.

2. Privacy Concerns: Collecting and storing student data raises significant privacy concerns, and it is important for schools and educational institutions to have strong data privacy policies in place to protect student data.

3. Teacher Training: AI-enabled personalized learning environments require teachers to have a high degree of technological proficiency and data literacy. Many teachers may require additional training to effectively integrate these technologies into their teaching practice.

4. Overreliance on Technology: There is a risk that AI-enabled personalized learning environments could lead to an overreliance on technology and a reduction in human interaction in the classroom. It is

important for educators to strike a balance between technology and traditional teaching methods.

AI-Enabled Personalized Learning Environments in Action:

Several organizations and institutions are already using AI-enabled personalized learning environments to improve student outcomes. For example, the Summit Learning Program is a personalized learning platform that has been adopted by more than 300 schools across the United States. The platform uses AI to create personalized learning paths for each student, and provides real-time feedback on their progress. Students using the Summit Learning Program have demonstrated significant gains in math and reading proficiency.

Another benefit of AI-enabled personalized learning environments is that they can help educators and school administrators identify at-risk students and provide timely interventions to support them. By monitoring students' progress in real-time and using machine learning algorithms to analyze their behavior and performance data, the system can detect patterns and indicators of students who are struggling or disengaged. This information can then be used to provide personalized support, such as targeted interventions, additional resources, or one-on-one tutoring, to help the student get back on track.

Moreover, AI-enabled personalized learning environments can also help reduce the workload of educators by automating certain tasks and providing them with insights and recommendations based on the data collected by the system. For instance, the system can automatically grade assignments and exams, freeing up the teacher's time to focus on more important tasks such as lesson planning, creating engaging content, and providing personalized feedback to students.

However, despite the numerous benefits, there are also challenges and limitations to implementing AI-enabled personalized learning environments. One challenge is the need for large amounts of high-quality data to train the machine learning algorithms. The more data the system has access to, the more accurate and effective it will be in providing personalized learning experiences. This requires a robust data infrastructure and the ability to collect, store, and analyze data in a secure and ethical manner.

Another challenge is the potential for bias and discrimination in the algorithms used by the system. Machine learning algorithms can only be as unbiased as the data they are trained on, and if the data reflects biases or stereotypes, the algorithm will also reproduce these biases. Therefore, it is crucial to ensure that the data used to train the system is diverse, inclusive, and representative of all students.

Furthermore, the use of AI-enabled personalized learning environments raises important ethical and privacy concerns. As these systems collect and analyze large amounts of student data, there is a risk of privacy violations and data breaches. It is crucial to implement robust security and privacy policies to protect student data and ensure that it is used only for educational purpose

Intelligent Tutoring Systems

Intelligent Tutoring Systems (ITS) are a type of educational technology that leverages artificial intelligence (AI) techniques to provide personalized learning experiences to students. The goal of ITS is to simulate the guidance and support that a human tutor would provide, but on a larger scale and with greater efficiency. The system provides real-time feedback, adapts to the student's progress, and offers additional resources to support their learning.

History of Intelligent Tutoring Systems

The roots of ITS can be traced back to the work of computer scientist and cognitive psychologist John Anderson in the 1980s. Anderson developed a cognitive architecture known as ACT-R, which he used to create intelligent tutors for subjects like algebra and physics. His work inspired a wave of research in the field of cognitive science, and over time, the concept of ITS evolved into a more sophisticated and effective tool for education.

Today, ITS has become a mainstream application of AI in education, with many commercial and academic systems in use around the world. The field continues to evolve, with ongoing research focused on improving the effectiveness of ITS and expanding its capabilities.

ITS is grounded in several theoretical frameworks, including cognitive science, learning theory, and artificial intelligence. These frameworks provide a basis for understanding how learners acquire knowledge, how feedback and scaffolding can support learning, and how intelligent algorithms can be used to optimize the learning process.

One of the key principles underlying ITS is the idea of scaffolding, which is the process of providing support to learners as they work through a task. Scaffolding can take many forms, including hints, explanations, and feedback, and its goal is to help learners move from a state of dependence to independence.

Another important concept in ITS is adaptive learning, which refers to the system's ability to adjust its instruction to meet the needs of individual learners. This involves assessing the learner's prior knowledge, monitoring their progress, and adjusting the level of difficulty of the content and tasks presented.

Benefits of Intelligent Tutoring Systems

Intelligent Tutoring Systems offer several benefits over traditional classroom instruction, including:

1. Personalized Learning: ITS offers a personalized learning experience that is tailored to the needs and abilities of individual learners. This helps to ensure that learners are challenged but not overwhelmed, and that they receive the support they need to succeed.
2. Immediate Feedback: ITS provides immediate feedback to learners, allowing them to correct their mistakes and reinforce their understanding of the material. This is particularly important in subjects like math and science, where accuracy is critical.
3. Flexibility: ITS is flexible and can be used in a variety of settings, including traditional classrooms, online courses, and distance learning programs. This makes it a versatile tool that can be adapted to meet the needs of different learners and educators.

4. Efficiency: ITS is more efficient than traditional classroom instruction, as it can provide personalized instruction and feedback to large numbers of students simultaneously. This can help to reduce the workload of educators and make learning more efficient for students.

Challenges and Limitations of Intelligent Tutoring Systems

While ITS offers many benefits, there are also some challenges and limitations that need to be considered, including:

1. Cost: Developing and implementing an ITS can be expensive, particularly for smaller educational institutions. This can limit the availability of ITS to only the most well-funded institutions.
2. Technical Complexity: ITS involves complex AI algorithms and requires significant technical expertise to develop and maintain. This can make it difficult for educators and schools with limited technical resources to implement.
3. Data Privacy and Security: ITS involves collecting and analyzing large amounts of student data, which raises concerns about

privacy and security. It is important to ensure that appropriate measures are in place to protect student data and ensure that it is used ethically.

4. Limited Subject Matter: While ITS can be effective in subjects like math and science, it may be less effective in subjects that rely more heavily on discussion and debate, such as philosophy and literature.

5. Lack of Human Interaction: While ITS can provide personalized instruction and feedback, it lacks the human element that is often critical for effective learning. Students may miss out on the benefits of face-to-face interactions with teachers and peers, which can be important for social and emotional development.

Intelligent Tutoring Systems (ITS) in Action

There are many different types of ITS in use today, each with its own strengths and weaknesses. Among the most common forms of ITS are:

1. Math Tutoring Systems: Math tutoring systems are among the most widely used types of ITS. They provide students with

personalized instruction and feedback on topics like algebra, geometry, and calculus.

2. Language Tutoring Systems: Language tutoring systems are designed to help students learn a new language, providing personalized instruction and feedback on grammar, vocabulary, and pronunciation.

3. Science Tutoring Systems: Science tutoring systems can be used to teach a wide range of topics, including physics, chemistry, and biology. They provide students with interactive simulations and feedback on their understanding of scientific concepts.

4. Programming Tutoring Systems: Programming tutoring systems are designed to help students learn to code, providing personalized instruction and feedback on topics like syntax, algorithms, and data structures.

Implementing Intelligent Tutoring Systems: Best Practices and Strategies

When implementing an ITS, it is important to follow best practices and strategies to ensure its effectiveness. Among the important techniques to examine are:

1. Choosing the Right System: There are many different types of ITS available, each with its own strengths and weaknesses. It is important to choose a system that is appropriate for the subject matter and the needs of the learners.

2. Providing Adequate Training: Educators and students will need adequate training to effectively use an ITS. This may involve providing training on the technical aspects of the system, as well as on the best practices for using it effectively.

3. Establishing Clear Learning Goals: It is important to establish clear learning goals for the use of an ITS. This may involve setting goals for specific skills or competencies, as well as establishing metrics for measuring progress.

4. Incorporating Feedback: ITS should provide students with frequent feedback on their progress, as well as on the effectiveness of the system itself. This feedback can be used to improve the system over time and to tailor instruction to the needs of individual learners.

5. Ensuring Privacy and Security: ITS involves collecting and analyzing large amounts of student data, which raises concerns about privacy and security. It is important to

ensure that appropriate measures are in place to protect student data and ensure that it is used ethically.

Chatbots and Conversational Agents in Education

Chatbots and conversational agents have become increasingly popular in education, as they provide a new way for students to interact with educational content and for educators to engage with their students. With the help of artificial intelligence (AI), chatbots and conversational agents can be designed to understand natural language and respond to student inquiries in real-time. In this article, we will explore the use of chatbots and conversational agents in education, their benefits, challenges, and limitations, as well as some best practices and case studies.

What are Chatbots and Conversational Agents?

Chatbots and conversational agents are computer programs designed to simulate human conversation through text or voice interactions. They are built using natural language processing (NLP) and machine learning algorithms, which enable them to understand and interpret human language. Chatbots and conversational agents can be programmed to provide information, answer questions, and offer assistance in a variety of contexts.

In education, chatbots and conversational agents are used to support student learning and provide personalized assistance. They can be integrated into learning management systems (LMS), mobile apps, or websites to provide students with immediate feedback and support. Chatbots and conversational agents can also be used to automate administrative tasks, such as answering frequently asked questions or providing scheduling information.

Benefits of Chatbots and Conversational Agents in Education

One of the main benefits of chatbots and conversational agents in education is their ability to provide personalized support to students. By understanding and interpreting natural language, chatbots and conversational agents can offer tailored assistance to each student, helping them to address their individual learning needs.

Another benefit of chatbots and conversational agents is their availability. They can be accessed at any time and from any location, making them an ideal tool for distance learning or self-directed study. Chatbots and conversational agents can also provide immediate feedback and support, which can help students to stay engaged and motivated.

Furthermore, chatbots and conversational agents can help to reduce the workload of educators. By automating routine tasks, such as answering frequently asked questions, chatbots and conversational agents can free up time for educators to focus on more complex tasks, such as designing curriculum or providing one-on-one support to students.

Challenges and Limitations of Chatbots and Conversational Agents in Education

While chatbots and conversational agents offer many benefits to education, there are also some challenges and limitations to consider. One of the main challenges is ensuring that the chatbot or conversational agent is accurate and reliable. If the chatbot or conversational agent provides incorrect information or misinterprets student inquiries, it can lead to confusion and frustration.

Another challenge is ensuring that the chatbot or conversational agent is accessible to all students. Students with disabilities, such as visual impairments, may have difficulty using a chatbot or conversational agent that relies on text or visual cues.

Additionally, there is a concern that chatbots and conversational agents may replace human interaction in education. While chatbots and conversational agents can provide personalized assistance and immediate feedback, they cannot replace the value of human interaction and the emotional support that educators can provide.

Best Practices for Implementing Chatbots and Conversational Agents in Education

To ensure that chatbots and conversational agents are effective in education, there are several best practices to consider:

1. Identify clear objectives: Before implementing a chatbot or conversational agent, it is important to identify clear objectives for its use. This will help to ensure that the chatbot or conversational agent is designed to meet specific learning goals.
2. Ensure accuracy and reliability: It is important to ensure that the chatbot or conversational agent is accurate and

reliable. This can be achieved through rigorous testing and ongoing monitoring.

3. Ensure accessibility: Chatbots and conversational agents should be designed to be accessible to all students, including those with disabilities. This can be achieved through the use of alternative input and output modalities, such as speech recognition and text-to-speech conversion.

4. Incorporate human interaction: While chatbots and conversational agents can provide valuable assistance, they should not replace human interaction. It is important to ensure that students have access to human support when needed.

5. Monitor and evaluate: It is important to monitor and evaluate the effectiveness of chatbots and conversational agents in education. This can be achieved through user feedback, performance metrics, and other evaluation methods.

Case Studies: Successful Applications of Chatbots and Conversational Agents in Education

There are many successful applications of chatbots and conversational agents in education. Here are a few examples:

1. Duolingo: Duolingo is a language learning platform that uses a chatbot to simulate conversations with native speakers. The chatbot provides immediate feedback and personalized support to help students improve their language skills.

2. Carnegie Mellon University: Carnegie Mellon University uses a chatbot to provide personalized support to students enrolled in online courses. The chatbot answers frequently asked questions and provides assistance with assignments and assessments.

3. Georgia State University: Georgia State University uses a chatbot to provide personalized support to students with financial aid questions. The chatbot provides real-time answers to common questions and helps students navigate the financial aid process.

4. San Francisco State University: San Francisco State University uses a chatbot to provide personalized support to students with disabilities. The chatbot provides assistance with accommodations, technology support, and other services.

Automated Essay Scoring

Automated Essay Scoring (AES) is the process of using computer programs to evaluate and score student essays. AES has been gaining popularity in education due to its potential to save time and resources, provide more objective scoring, and increase consistency in grading. However, there are also concerns about the accuracy and fairness of AES, as well as its impact on teaching and learning. In this article, we will explore the history, theoretical frameworks, benefits, challenges, and future of AES.

History of Automated Essay Scoring

The use of computers to score essays dates back to the 1960s, when researchers at Educational Testing Service (ETS) developed Project Essay Grader, a program that used patterns of vocabulary and sentence structure to grade essays. However, the limitations of early AES systems, such as their inability to capture the complexity of writing, led to a decline in their use in the 1970s and 1980s.

In the 1990s, advances in Natural Language Processing (NLP) and machine learning led to the development of more sophisticated AES systems. These systems used algorithms to analyze various aspects of an essay, such as syntax, semantics, and discourse, and compare them to a pre-established set of criteria or a corpus of previously scored essays. Since then, AES has become more widespread, with many standardized tests and educational institutions using it to grade essays.

Theoretical Frameworks for Automated Essay Scoring

There are several theoretical frameworks for AES, each with its own approach to evaluating essays. One popular framework is the e-rater scoring engine, developed by ETS. The e-rater system uses a combination of machine learning algorithms and rule-based heuristics to evaluate essays based on a pre-established set of criteria, such as organization, development, and language use. The system compares the essay to a corpus of previously scored essays and generates a score based on the similarities and differences between them.

Another framework is the Intelligent Essay Assessor (IEA), developed by Pearson Education. The IEA system uses Latent Semantic Analysis (LSA) to analyze essays based on their meaning and coherence. The system compares the essay to a pre-established set of criteria and generates a score based on the degree of similarity between the essay and the criteria.

Benefits of Automated Essay Scoring

There are several potential benefits of AES in education. These include:

1. Time-saving: AES can save time for educators by automating the grading process, allowing them to focus on other aspects of teaching and learning.
2. Objectivity: AES can provide more objective grading by removing the potential for human bias or subjectivity in grading.
3. Consistency: AES can increase consistency in grading by providing the same criteria and standards for all essays.
4. Feedback: AES can provide immediate feedback to students, allowing them to learn from their mistakes and improve their writing skills.

5. Accessibility: AES can make grading more accessible by providing consistent and reliable grading for large numbers of essays, regardless of their location or time zone.

Challenges and Limitations of Automated Essay Scoring

Despite the potential benefits of AES, there are also several challenges and limitations associated with its use. These include:

1. Accuracy: The accuracy of AES can be affected by the quality of the essay and the complexity of the writing. AES may struggle with evaluating more creative or nuanced writing.
2. Fairness: AES may not be able to capture all aspects of writing, such as tone, style, and voice, which can lead to inaccurate or unfair grading.
3. Feedback: AES may not provide detailed or personalized feedback to students, which can limit their ability to learn and improve their writing skills.
4. Cost: AES can be expensive to implement and maintain, requiring significant

investment in hardware, software, and training.

5. Ethical concerns: There are ethical concerns regarding the use of AES, such as the potential for the system to be biased or discriminatory, particularly against certain groups or types of writing.
6. Pedagogical concerns: The use of AES may have an impact on teaching and learning, such as reducing the focus on feedback and revision, and encouraging formulaic or template-based writing.

AI-Powered Adaptive Learning Systems

One way to address the limitations of AES is to integrate it into AI-powered adaptive learning systems, which can personalize instruction and support student learning in real-time. Adaptive learning systems use data analytics and machine learning algorithms to tailor instruction to each student's unique needs, based on their performance and progress. AES can be used as a component of these systems to provide feedback and guidance on students' writing, as well as to generate data for further analysis and improvement.

AI-Enabled Personalized Learning Environments

Another approach to integrating AES into education is through AI-enabled personalized learning environments. These environments use machine learning algorithms to adapt to each student's learning style, preferences, and needs, providing customized instruction, feedback, and resources. AES can be used within these environments to provide students with immediate feedback on their writing and to guide them towards resources and activities that can help them improve their writing skills.

Intelligent Tutoring Systems

Intelligent tutoring systems (ITS) are another application of AI in education that can incorporate AES. ITS use machine learning algorithms to provide personalized and adaptive instruction to students, based on their performance and needs. AES can be used within these systems to evaluate and score students' writing, providing feedback and guidance to help them improve their skills.

Chatbots and Conversational Agents in Education

Chatbots and conversational agents are AI-powered tools that can assist with various aspects of education, such as answering questions, providing feedback, and guiding students through learning activities. AES can be integrated into chatbots and conversational agents to provide students with feedback on their writing, as well as to guide them towards resources and activities that can help them improve their writing skills.

Grading Automation and Analytics

Another application of AES in education is grading automation and analytics. AES can be used to automate the grading of large numbers of essays, such as those submitted for standardized tests, saving time and resources for educators. AES can also generate data analytics on students' writing, such as identifying common errors and areas for improvement, which can inform instruction and curriculum development.

AI-Assisted Curriculum Development

AES can also be used to assist with curriculum development, by analyzing large datasets of essays to identify trends and patterns in writing. This information can inform the development of writing standards, curricula, and instructional materials.

AI in STEM Education

While AES has primarily been used in language arts and writing instruction, it can also be applied to STEM education. AES can evaluate students' writing in STEM subjects, such as scientific writing or technical reports, providing feedback and guidance on clarity, organization, and other aspects of effective writing in these fields.

AI-Enabled Language Learning

AES can also be used in language learning instruction, such as evaluating and scoring students' writing in second language acquisition. AES can provide feedback on grammar, vocabulary, and syntax, as well as evaluate students' writing proficiency over time.

AI and Special Education

AES can also be applied to special education, such as evaluating and scoring the writing of students with disabilities or other learning challenges. AES can provide objective and consistent grading, as well as personalized feedback and support for students who may struggle with writing.

Ethics and Privacy Concerns in AES

As with any application of AI in education, there are ethical and privacy concerns regarding the use of AES. One concern is the potential for bias or discrimination in grading, particularly against certain groups or types of writing. Another concern is the privacy and security of student data, as AES requires the collection and analysis of large amounts of student writing. It is important for educators and developers to address these concerns and ensure that AES is used in a responsible and ethical manner.

One potential solution to these concerns is the use of transparent and explainable AI, which allows users to understand how the system works and how it makes decisions. This can help to mitigate the potential for bias or discrimination in grading, as well as ensure that students' privacy is protected.

Future of AES in Education

The future of AES in education is promising, as the technology continues to improve and become more sophisticated. Advances in natural language processing and machine learning algorithms are making AES more accurate and reliable, as well as more adaptable to different writing genres and contexts.

One area of future development for AES is the incorporation of more advanced features, such as semantic analysis and discourse-level analysis. These features would allow AES to evaluate not only the surface-level aspects of writing, such as grammar and syntax, but also the deeper structure and meaning of the text.

Another area of development is the integration of AES into more complex AI-powered systems, such as those that incorporate chatbots, adaptive learning, and analytics. By combining AES with other AI tools, educators can provide students with more personalized and effective instruction, as well as gain insights into student learning that can inform future instruction and curriculum development.

Best Practices for Implementing AES

When implementing AES in education, there are several best practices that educators and developers should follow:

1. Use transparent and explainable AI to mitigate concerns about bias and discrimination.
2. Provide students with opportunities for revision and feedback, in addition to the automated feedback provided by AES.
3. Use AES in conjunction with other forms of assessment, such as human grading or peer review, to ensure the accuracy and fairness of grading.
4. Ensure that AES is used as a tool for instruction and support, rather than as a replacement for human teachers.

Successful Applications of AES in Education

There have been several successful applications of AES in education, demonstrating the potential of this technology to improve writing instruction and student learning outcomes. One example is the use of AES in the Advanced Placement (AP) English Language and Composition exam, which has been shown to be as reliable and accurate as human graders. Another example is the use of AES in Massive Open Online Courses (MOOCs), where it has been used to provide immediate feedback and support to students on a large scale.

Curriculum development is a complex process that involves designing educational programs to meet the needs of students. Traditionally, curriculum development has been a labor-intensive and time-consuming process, with educators spending hours researching, designing, and testing different teaching materials and methods. However, with the advent of artificial intelligence (AI) technologies, this process has become more efficient and effective. AI-assisted curriculum development refers to the use of AI technologies to automate, enhance, and optimize the process of designing, developing, and implementing educational programs.

The Benefits of AI-Assisted Curriculum Development

AI-assisted curriculum development offers several benefits that can improve the quality of education for students. These benefits include:

1. Personalization: AI technologies can analyze student data and provide insights into their learning styles, strengths, and weaknesses. This information can be used to tailor the curriculum to meet the

individual needs of students, providing them with personalized learning experiences that can improve engagement, motivation, and retention.

2. Efficiency: AI technologies can automate time-consuming tasks such as data analysis, content creation, and assessment. This can reduce the workload of educators and allow them to focus on more meaningful tasks, such as interacting with students and providing personalized support.

3. Flexibility: AI technologies can provide educators with real-time feedback and insights on student progress, allowing them to adjust the curriculum and teaching methods as needed. This flexibility can help educators adapt to the changing needs of students and provide them with the best possible learning experience.

4. Scalability: AI technologies can help educators create and deliver educational content to a large number of students in a scalable manner. This can reduce the cost of education and increase access to high-quality educational programs.

5. Improved Learning Outcomes: By leveraging data insights and providing personalized learning experiences, AI-

assisted curriculum development can improve learning outcomes for students. This can lead to higher levels of student achievement, better retention rates, and improved student engagement.

AI-Assisted Curriculum Development Tools and Techniques

There are several AI-assisted curriculum development tools and techniques that educators can use to create personalized and effective educational programs. These include:

1. Learning Analytics: Learning analytics is the process of collecting, analyzing, and using student data to improve learning outcomes. AI technologies can be used to analyze large data sets and provide insights into student performance, behavior, and engagement. This information can be used to tailor the curriculum to meet the individual needs of students and improve learning outcomes.

2. Natural Language Processing (NLP): Natural language processing is a branch of AI that deals with the interaction between computers and humans in natural language. NLP can be used to analyze text-

based educational materials and provide insights into the readability, complexity, and effectiveness of the content. This information can be used to improve the quality of educational materials and make them more accessible to students.

3. Intelligent Tutoring Systems (ITS): Intelligent tutoring systems are AI technologies that provide personalized feedback and guidance to students. ITS can analyze student data and provide real-time feedback on their performance, helping them improve their skills and knowledge. ITS can also adapt to the individual needs of students, providing them with personalized learning experiences.

4. Content Creation: AI technologies can be used to create educational content such as quizzes, assessments, and interactive learning activities. These tools can automate the process of content creation, reducing the workload of educators and providing students with high-quality educational materials.

5. Adaptive Learning: Adaptive learning is a teaching method that uses AI technologies to adjust the curriculum and teaching methods to meet the individual needs of students. AI technologies can analyze

student data and provide insights into their learning styles, strengths, and weaknesses. This information can be used to tailor the curriculum to meet the individual needs of students, providing them with personalized learning experiences.

Challenges and Limitations of AI-Assisted Curriculum Development

While AI-assisted curriculum development offers several benefits, it also faces several challenges and limitations that must be addressed. These challenges include:

1. Bias: AI technologies can be biased based on the data they are trained on. This can lead to biased educational materials and assessments that do not accurately represent the diversity of students. Educators must ensure that AI technologies are trained on diverse and inclusive data sets to avoid bias.

2. Data Privacy: AI technologies require access to student data to provide personalized learning experiences. However, this data must be protected to ensure student privacy. Educators must ensure that student data is collected and used in a responsible and ethical manner.

3. Technical Complexity: AI technologies can be complex and difficult to implement. Educators must have the necessary technical expertise to implement and use AI technologies effectively.

4. Lack of Human Interaction: AI technologies can automate many tasks, but they cannot replace the human interaction that is essential to education. Educators must ensure that AI technologies are used in conjunction with human interaction to provide students with a well-rounded learning experience.

5. Cost: Implementing AI technologies can be expensive, especially for smaller educational institutions. Educators must consider the cost-benefit analysis of implementing AI technologies and ensure that the benefits outweigh the costs.

Implementing AI-Assisted Curriculum Development: Best Practices and Strategies

To successfully implement AI-assisted curriculum development, educators must follow best practices and strategies. These include:

1. Starting Small: Educators should start with small pilot projects to test the effectiveness

of AI technologies before scaling up to larger projects.

2. Collaboration: Educators should collaborate with AI experts and other educators to develop and implement AI technologies effectively.

3. Professional Development: Educators must receive professional development training to effectively use and implement AI technologies.

4. Data Privacy: Educators must ensure that student data is collected and used in a responsible and ethical manner. This includes obtaining student consent and protecting their privacy.

5. Transparency: Educators must ensure that AI technologies are transparent and explainable. Students and educators must understand how AI technologies are being used and how they are making decisions.

6. Evaluation: Educators must evaluate the effectiveness of AI technologies regularly to ensure that they are meeting the needs of students.

Case Studies: Successful Applications of AI-Assisted Curriculum Development

There have been several successful applications of AI-assisted curriculum development in education. These include:

1. Carnegie Learning: Carnegie Learning is an adaptive learning platform that uses AI technologies to personalize the curriculum to meet the individual needs of students. Carnegie Learning has been shown to improve student learning outcomes in math and science.

2. Knewton: Knewton is an adaptive learning platform that uses AI technologies to analyze student data and provide personalized learning experiences. Knewton has been used in several educational institutions to improve student learning outcomes.

3. IBM Watson Education: IBM Watson Education is an AI-powered education platform that provides personalized learning experiences for students. IBM Watson Education has been used in several educational institutions to improve student learning outcomes.

4. Duolingo: Duolingo is a language learning platform that uses AI technologies to personalize the curriculum and provide real-time feedback to students. Duolingo has been shown to improve language learning outcomes for students.

Grading Automation and Analytics

One of the most significant benefits of Artificial Intelligence (AI) in education is its ability to automate grading and provide data-driven insights to improve student learning outcomes. Grading automation, in particular, has the potential to revolutionize the way we assess and evaluate student performance, saving teachers significant amounts of time and effort while ensuring consistency and fairness in grading.

Grading automation tools use algorithms and machine learning models to evaluate student work, such as quizzes, assignments, and exams. These tools can analyze text, image, and even audio-based assignments to provide a score or grade to students. By automating grading, teachers can focus on providing more valuable feedback and support to their students, rather than spending hours grading repetitive assignments.

1. Increased Efficiency and Consistency

Grading automation can save teachers countless hours of grading and scoring, freeing them up to focus on other important tasks, such as lesson planning, individualized instruction, and student support. It can also provide consistent and objective grading, eliminating the potential for biases and variations in grading between different teachers or classes.

2. More Frequent and Timely Feedback

Grading automation tools can provide real-time feedback to students, allowing them to receive immediate feedback on their assignments and adjust their learning accordingly. This feedback can also be used to help teachers identify areas where students are struggling, providing insights into where they may need additional support or instruction.

3. Improved Learning Outcomes

Grading automation tools can provide teachers with valuable data on student performance, including trends, strengths, and weaknesses. This data can be used to identify areas where students need additional support, adjust teaching strategies and materials, and create more personalized learning experiences that better meet the needs of individual students.

Challenges and Limitations of Grading Automation and Analytics

While grading automation has many potential benefits, it also has its share of challenges and limitations that must be addressed to ensure its effectiveness and accuracy.

1. Limited Ability to Evaluate Complex Work

Grading automation tools are most effective when evaluating simple assignments, such as multiple-choice questions or short answer responses. However, they may struggle to accurately evaluate more complex assignments, such as essays, research papers, or creative projects. These types of assignments require a deeper understanding of the content and context, making it challenging for grading automation tools to provide accurate and meaningful feedback.

2. Difficulty in Assessing Creativity and Critical Thinking

Grading automation tools may struggle to accurately evaluate assignments that require creativity, critical thinking, or problem-solving skills. These types of assignments are highly subjective and often require human judgment to assess accurately. As such, grading automation tools may not provide the same level of feedback as human graders.

3. Risk of Bias and Error

Grading automation tools are only as accurate as the algorithms and machine learning models they use. If the models are not properly calibrated or trained, they may produce biased or inaccurate results, leading to unfair or inconsistent grading. Additionally, grading automation tools may struggle to recognize and evaluate unique writing styles, dialects, or cultural differences, leading to errors in grading.

Best Practices for Grading Automation and Analytics

To ensure the effectiveness and accuracy of grading automation tools, educators should consider the following best practices:

1. Understand the Limitations of Grading Automation

Educators should be aware of the limitations of grading automation and avoid using these tools to evaluate complex assignments that require human judgment. Instead, they should focus on using these tools to grade simple assignments, such as multiple-choice questions or short answer responses, and to provide real-time feedback to students.

2. Train and Calibrate the Machine Learning Models

To ensure the accuracy of grading automation tools, educators should train and calibrate the machine learning models regularly. This will help to eliminate biases and errors and ensure that the grading is fair and consistent across all students and assignments.

3. Use Multiple Grading Automation Tools

To further increase the accuracy of grading automation, educators should use multiple grading automation tools and compare the results to ensure consistency and accuracy across different tools. This can help to identify any errors or biases in the grading algorithms and ensure that all students receive a fair and accurate grade.

4. Provide Additional Feedback and Support

While grading automation tools can provide valuable feedback to students, educators should still provide additional feedback and support to help students improve their learning outcomes. This can include personalized instruction, one-on-one meetings, or additional resources to help students better understand the material.

5. Communicate with Students and Parents

Educators should communicate with students and parents about the use of grading automation tools and how they are being used to evaluate student performance. This can help to build trust and transparency and ensure that everyone is aware of how grading is being done.

Successful Applications of Grading Automation and Analytics

There are many successful applications of grading automation and analytics in education. For example, Turnitin is a popular grading automation tool used by many schools and universities to check student work for plagiarism and provide feedback on writing style, grammar, and punctuation. Similarly, Edmentum's Study Island platform uses machine learning to grade multiple-choice and short answer questions and provide real-time feedback to students.

In addition, many schools and universities are using learning management systems (LMS) such as Blackboard, Canvas, and Moodle to automate grading and provide data-driven insights into student performance. These systems allow educators to grade assignments online, provide real-time feedback to students, and track student progress over time.

AI in STEM Education

Artificial intelligence (AI) has profoundly revolutionized several industries, including education. In STEM (Science, Technology, Engineering, and Mathematics) education, AI is increasingly gaining attention as a tool for enhancing teaching and learning experiences. STEM education is critical in today's world, as it plays a crucial role in preparing the future workforce and driving technological advancements. In this article, we will explore the role of AI in STEM education, its benefits, challenges, and future prospects.

AI Applications in STEM Education

AI has various applications in STEM education, and here are some of the most promising ones:

1. Intelligent Tutoring Systems

Intelligent Tutoring Systems (ITS) are AI-powered platforms that offer personalized learning experiences to students. ITS utilizes various techniques such as natural language processing, machine learning, and data analytics to provide immediate feedback to students, track their progress, and offer personalized recommendations based on their learning style and performance. ITS is particularly useful in STEM education, as it allows students to learn at their own pace and address their knowledge gaps effectively.

2. Robotics and Automation

AI-powered robots and automation systems are increasingly becoming a common feature in STEM classrooms. These systems allow students to learn and experiment with robotics and automation technologies, which are essential skills for the future workforce. For instance, students can learn how to code robots to perform specific tasks or automate repetitive tasks using machine learning algorithms.

3. Virtual and Augmented Reality

Virtual and Augmented Reality (VR/AR) technologies offer immersive learning experiences that allow students to interact with complex STEM concepts in a more engaging and interactive manner. For example, VR/AR simulations can help students explore complex scientific concepts such as the human body, chemistry, and physics, in a more interactive and engaging way.

4. Data Analytics and Visualization

Data analytics and visualization tools offer students a powerful way to explore and analyze complex data sets, which are essential skills in the STEM field. AI-powered data analytics tools can help students understand complex concepts such as statistics, machine learning, and data mining, in a more intuitive and interactive way.

Benefits of AI in STEM Education

AI has various benefits in STEM education, and here are some of the most significant ones:

1. Personalized Learning

AI-powered platforms such as Intelligent Tutoring Systems offer personalized learning experiences to students. This allows students to learn at their own pace, address their knowledge gaps, and receive immediate feedback on their performance.

2. Improved Student Engagement

AI-powered tools such as VR/AR simulations and robotics offer more engaging and interactive learning experiences that capture students' attention and stimulate their interest in STEM subjects.

3. Enhanced Learning Outcomes

AI-powered platforms and tools offer students a more effective and efficient way of learning STEM subjects. For instance, students can learn and experiment with robotics and automation technologies, which are essential skills for the future workforce.

4. Improved Accessibility

AI-powered platforms and tools offer more accessible learning experiences to students, regardless of their geographical location or physical disabilities.

Challenges and Limitations of AI in STEM Education

Despite its many benefits, AI also presents various challenges and limitations in STEM education, and here are some of the most significant ones:

1. Cost

AI-powered platforms and tools can be expensive to develop, implement, and maintain. This can limit their accessibility to schools and students with limited financial resources.

2. Privacy and Security

   AI-powered platforms and tools collect and analyze large amounts of data, which can pose significant privacy and security risks to students' personal information.

3. Ethical Concerns

   AI-powered platforms and tools raise various ethical concerns, such as the potential for bias and discrimination in decision-making processes.

4. Technical Expertise

   AI-powered platforms and tools require technical expertise to develop, implement, and maintain. This can limit their accessibility to schools and students with limited technical expertise.

5. Lack of Human Interaction

   AI-powered platforms and tools can reduce the human interaction and personalization in the learning experience. This can limit the development of critical thinking, problem-solving, and interpersonal skills.

6. Inadequate Training

Teachers and educators require adequate training and support to effectively use and integrate AI-powered platforms and tools into their teaching practices.

Here are some of the most promising AI-powered STEM education tools and platforms:

1. Carnegie Learning

    Carnegie Learning is an AI-powered platform that offers personalized learning experiences in math and science subjects. The platform utilizes various techniques such as machine learning and data analytics to offer immediate feedback to students, track their progress, and provide personalized recommendations.

2. Labster

    Labster is an AI-powered platform that offers virtual and interactive science lab simulations. The platform utilizes VR/AR technologies to offer immersive and engaging learning experiences to students.

3. RoboGarden

RoboGarden is an AI-powered platform that offers coding and robotics courses for K-12 students. The platform utilizes gamification and personalized learning techniques to make coding and robotics more engaging and accessible to students.

4. Smart Sparrow

Smart Sparrow is an AI-powered platform that offers adaptive and personalized learning experiences in STEM subjects. The platform utilizes various techniques such as natural language processing, machine learning, and data analytics to provide immediate feedback to students, track their progress, and offer personalized recommendations.

5. Code.org

Code.org is a nonprofit organization that offers free coding courses for K-12 students. The organization utilizes various techniques such as gamification and interactive learning to make coding more engaging and accessible to students.

Future of AI in Education: Trends and Predictions

The integration of artificial intelligence (AI) in education has opened up new avenues of learning and has transformed traditional educational practices. With the ever-evolving landscape of AI and machine learning, the future of AI in education is promising. In this article, we will explore the trends and predictions for the future of AI in education.

Personalized Learning

Personalized learning is one of the most important educational developments. With the help of AI, educators can create personalized learning experiences tailored to the needs of each student. AI-enabled adaptive learning platforms can analyze student data and develop individualized learning paths. These platforms can track students' progress and provide targeted interventions to help them overcome their learning challenges.

Adaptive Learning

Adaptive learning is a process in which the system adapts to the learner's knowledge and performance level. This approach is particularly beneficial for students with different learning styles, strengths, and weaknesses. Adaptive learning platforms can adjust the level of difficulty of the content, the pace of learning, and the type of activities based on each student's performance.

Virtual Reality

Cyberspace (VR) is a novel technology that is increasingly being used in education. With VR, students can explore complex concepts and theories in a simulated environment. This immersive experience can help students retain knowledge better and develop a deeper understanding of the subject matter. AI-powered VR systems can provide personalized feedback and adaptive learning paths to help students achieve their learning goals.

Gamification

Gamification is the use of game design elements and mechanics in non-game contexts, such as education. Gamification has the potential to make learning more interesting, motivating, and fun. AI can be used to develop personalized games that adapt to each student's learning needs and progress.

Chatbots

Chatbots are AI-powered conversational agents that can interact with students in a natural language. Chatbots can provide instant feedback, answer questions, and offer personalized learning suggestions. Chatbots can also assist teachers in administrative tasks, such as grading assignments, tracking student progress, and scheduling appointments.

Predictive Analytics

The use of data, statistical algorithms, and machine learning approaches to find trends and forecast future events is known as predictive analytics. Predictive analytics may be used in education to examine student data and forecast academic achievement, learning obstacles, and future learning requirements. Predictive analytics may also assist instructors in developing individualised interventions and providing pupils with focused support.

Natural Language Processing

Natural Language Processing (NLP) is an area of artificial intelligence that deals with the interaction of computers and human language.

NLP can be used to analyze student writing and provide instant feedback on grammar, spelling, and syntax. NLP can also be used to analyze student discourse and identify patterns of interaction, such as dominance, participation, and engagement.

Robotics

Robotics is another emerging technology that is being used in education. Robotics can be used to teach coding, engineering, and problem-solving skills. AI-powered robots can also provide personalized feedback, adapt to each student's learning needs, and assist teachers in administrative tasks.

Blockchain

Blockchain is a decentralized, secure, and transparent ledger that can be used to store and share data. In education, blockchain can be used to store student records, certifications, and transcripts. Blockchain can provide a secure and tamper-proof way of verifying student credentials, which can be beneficial for students seeking employment or further education.

Cloud Computing

The distribution of computer services through the internet is known as cloud computing. Cloud computing can provide educators and students with access to a vast array of educational resources, tools, and applications. Cloud computing can also facilitate collaborative learning, enable personalized learning, and provide real-time feedback and assessment.

Successful Applications of AI in Education

Artificial Intelligence (AI) has become an essential tool in various fields, including education. AI technology has transformed the traditional ways of teaching and learning, allowing for more personalized and efficient education. In this article, we will explore some of the successful applications of AI in education through case studies.

1. Carnegie Learning

   Carnegie Learning is an education technology company that provides AI-powered math curriculums and adaptive learning solutions for K-12 schools. The company's adaptive learning system, MATHia, uses AI to provide personalized learning paths for each student, based on their strengths, weaknesses, and learning style.

   The AI algorithm behind MATHia uses cognitive and educational research to understand the student's knowledge gaps, identify misconceptions, and provide targeted feedback. The system also includes virtual math coaches that guide students through difficult concepts and provide support.

According to a study by the RAND Corporation, students who used MATHia for a full academic year showed significant improvement in their math skills compared to those who used traditional textbooks. The study also found that the more students used the system, the greater their improvement.

2. Duolingo

Duolingo is a language learning platform that uses AI to provide personalized learning experiences. The platform offers more than 40 language courses and has over 300 million users worldwide. Duolingo's AI algorithm uses machine learning to adapt to each learner's pace, progress, and learning style.

The AI system behind Duolingo analyzes the learner's performance and adjusts the difficulty level of the exercises accordingly. The platform also uses gamification techniques to keep learners motivated and engaged. For example, learners earn points and badges for completing lessons and can compete with friends on the leaderboard.

According to a study by the City University of New York, students who used Duolingo for 34 hours showed significant improvement in their

Spanish proficiency compared to those who used a traditional language textbook. The study also found that students who used Duolingo were more likely to continue learning the language after the study ended.

3. IBM Watson Education

IBM Watson Education is an AI-powered platform that provides personalized learning experiences and teacher support. The platform uses natural language processing (NLP) and machine learning to analyze student data, identify learning gaps, and provide targeted recommendations for teachers.

The AI system behind IBM Watson Education uses data from student assessments, teacher feedback, and other sources to provide personalized learning plans for each student. The platform also includes a virtual assistant, Teacher Advisor with Watson, that helps teachers find relevant resources and lesson plans for their classes.

According to a study by IBM, schools that used IBM Watson Education showed significant improvement in student performance and engagement compared to schools that did not use the platform. The study also found that teachers who used the platform reported feeling more confident and prepared in their teaching.

4. Gradescope

Gradescope is an AI-powered platform that streamlines the grading process for teachers and provides feedback for students. The platform uses machine learning to recognize and grade handwritten and typed responses, saving teachers time and reducing grading errors.

The AI system behind Gradescope uses computer vision to analyze students' handwriting and identify key elements of their responses, such as equations and diagrams. The platform also provides detailed analytics on student performance, allowing teachers to identify common mistakes and areas for improvement.

According to a study by the University of California, Berkeley, teachers who used Gradescope spent significantly less time grading assignments compared to those who used traditional methods. The study also found that students who received feedback through Gradescope showed improved performance on subsequent assignments.

5. ALEKS

ALEKS (Assessment and Learning in Knowledge Spaces) is an AI-powered platform that offers individualised math instruction to students in grades K-12 and higher education. The platform use adaptive questioning and evaluation to discover knowledge gaps in students and give targeted training.

The AI system behind ALEKS uses a mastery-based approach, meaning that students must demonstrate proficiency in a topic before moving on to the next one. The platform also includes virtual tutors that guide students through difficult concepts and provide feedback.

According to a study by the University of California, Los Angeles, students who used ALEKS for an entire academic year showed significant improvement in their math skills compared to those who used traditional textbooks. The study also found that students who used ALEKS were more likely to stay engaged and complete the course.

6. Knewton

Knewton is an adaptive learning platform that uses AI to provide personalized learning experiences for K-12 and higher education students. The platform uses machine learning to analyze student data, identify learning gaps, and provide targeted recommendations for teachers.

The AI system behind Knewton uses data from student assessments, engagement, and performance to create personalized learning paths for each student. The platform also includes virtual tutors that provide feedback and support.

According to a study by Arizona State University, students who used Knewton showed significant improvement in their performance compared to those who used traditional textbooks. The study also found that students who used Knewton were more likely to stay engaged and complete the course.

7. Coursera

Coursera is an online learning platform that offers courses from top universities and organizations worldwide. The platform uses AI to provide personalized learning experiences and support for students.

The AI system behind Coursera uses data from student assessments, engagement, and performance to create personalized learning paths for each student. The platform also includes virtual tutors that provide feedback and support.

According to a study by the University of Washington, students who used Coursera showed significant improvement in their performance compared to those who did not use the platform. The study also found that students who used Coursera were more likely to complete the course and receive a certificate.

The Role of Educators in AI-Enabled Education: The Importance of Human Interaction

Introduction

Artificial intelligence (AI) is changing the face of education by introducing innovative and efficient methods of learning. AI-powered education technologies like intelligent tutoring systems, personalized learning environments, and chatbots are providing students with personalized learning experiences and reducing the burden on teachers. However, the use of AI in education raises concerns about the role of educators in the learning process. This article will explore the role of educators in AI-enabled education and the importance of human interaction in the learning process.

The Role of Educators in AI-Enabled Education

The use of AI in education is not meant to replace human teachers but to support them in providing a personalized learning experience for each student. Educators have a critical role to play in designing and implementing AI-enabled education technologies. They must ensure that the AI-powered systems are aligned with the learning objectives and pedagogical approaches of the curriculum. Educators must also understand the limitations of AI and ensure that students receive a well-rounded education that includes social, emotional, and cognitive development.

The Importance of Human Interaction

While AI-powered education technologies provide a personalized learning experience, they cannot replace the human touch. Human interaction is essential for effective learning, especially in the social and emotional domains. Educators play a critical role in facilitating social interactions among students and promoting emotional well-being. They can provide feedback, guidance, and support to students, which AI systems cannot replace.

Educators can also help students develop critical thinking and problem-solving skills, which are essential for success in the 21st century. AI systems can provide students with answers and solutions to problems, but they cannot teach them how to think critically and creatively. Educators can provide students with challenging tasks that require them to apply their knowledge and skills in novel situations.

Furthermore, human interaction is essential for building relationships and creating a sense of community in the classroom. Educators can create a safe and inclusive learning environment where students feel valued and respected. They can encourage collaboration and teamwork among students and provide opportunities for them to learn from each other. These social interactions can help students develop important life skills such as communication, empathy, and leadership.

The Role of Educators in Assessing and Interpreting AI-Powered Learning Data

AI-powered education technologies generate vast amounts of data that can be used to assess student progress and provide personalized feedback. Educators have a critical role to play in interpreting and analyzing this data to make informed decisions about student learning. They must ensure that the data is accurate and reliable and use it to identify areas where students need additional support or challenge.

Educators can also use the data to assess the effectiveness of their teaching strategies and make adjustments as necessary. They can identify patterns in student learning and use this information to tailor their instruction to meet the needs of individual students.

Furthermore, educators can use the data generated by AI systems to communicate with parents and other stakeholders about student progress. They can provide detailed reports on student performance and use this information to engage parents in the learning process.

Best Practices for Integrating AI into Education

Integrating AI into education requires a collaborative effort between educators, administrators, and technology developers. Here are some best practices for integrating AI into education:

1. Involve Educators in the Development Process: Educators should be involved in the development process of AI-powered education technologies. They can provide valuable insights into the learning objectives and pedagogical approaches of the curriculum.

2. Ensure Alignment with Learning Objectives: AI-powered education technologies must be aligned with the learning objectives and pedagogical approaches of the curriculum. Educators

must ensure that the technologies support student learning and are not a distraction.

3. Provide Professional Development: Educators must receive professional development to learn how to use AI-powered education technologies effectively. They must understand the limitations of AI and ensure that students receive a well-rounded education that includes social, emotional development, critical thinking, and problem-solving.

4. Use AI to Enhance, Not Replace, Human Interaction: AI-powered education technologies should be used to enhance, not replace, human interaction. Educators must provide students with opportunities for social and emotional learning, critical thinking, and problem-solving.

5. Ensure Privacy and Security: AI-powered education technologies must ensure the privacy and security of student data. Educators and administrators must ensure that data is collected and used in compliance with privacy laws and regulations.

6. Evaluate Effectiveness: Educators must evaluate the effectiveness of AI-powered education technologies regularly. They

must use the data generated by these systems to inform their teaching strategies and make adjustments as necessary.

7. Communicate with Parents and Other Stakeholders: Educators must communicate with parents and other stakeholders about the use of AI in education. They must provide detailed reports on student progress and use this information to engage parents in the learning process.

Successful Applications of AI in Education

AI-powered education technologies are being used successfully in many countries around the world. Here are some examples:

1. Duolingo: Duolingo is an AI-powered language learning platform that provides personalized instruction based on the user's learning style and progress.

2. Carnegie Learning: Carnegie Learning is an intelligent tutoring system that provides personalized math instruction to students in grades 6-12. It uses adaptive learning algorithms to adjust instruction to the individual needs of each student.

3. Coursera: Coursera is an AI-powered web - based learning platform that offers courses from world-renowned colleges and institutes. It employs artificial intelligence to tailor education and deliver feedback to students.

4. Dreambox: Dreambox is an adaptive learning platform that provides personalized math instruction to students in grades K-8. It uses AI algorithms to adjust instruction based on the individual needs of each student.

Conclusion

In conclusion, AI in education has the potential to revolutionize the way we learn and teach. From early attempts to the current state, AI has come a long way in education. Theoretical frameworks, such as adaptive learning, personalized learning, and intelligent tutoring systems, have provided a foundation for the development of AI-powered education technologies.

AI in education offers several benefits, including improving learning outcomes, providing personalized learning experiences, and reducing administrative burdens. However, there are also challenges and limitations to the use of AI in education, including concerns about privacy and security, ethical considerations, and potential job displacement for educators.

Despite these challenges, successful applications of AI in education, such as Duolingo, Carnegie Learning, Coursera, and Dreambox, have demonstrated the potential for AI to provide personalized and effective learning experiences for students.

The role of educators in AI-enabled education cannot be overstated. Educators play a critical role in designing and implementing AI-powered education technologies, interpreting and analyzing learning data, and providing social and emotional support to students. The use of AI in education must be done in a way that enhances, not replaces, human interaction.

As AI in education continues to evolve, it is important for educators, policymakers, and other stakeholders to work together to ensure that the technology is used in a way that benefits students and improves education outcomes. By following best practices, evaluating effectiveness, and communicating with parents and stakeholders, educators can provide students with the best possible learning experience with the help of AI.

www.ingramcontent.com/pod-product-compliance
Lightning Source LLC
LaVergne TN
LVHW051702050326
832903LV00032B/3955